Who Do We Say That We Are?

Who Do We Say That We Are?

Christian Identity in a Multi-Religious World

Interreligious Dialogue
and Cooperation
World Council of Churches

**World Council
of Churches**
Publications

WHO DO WE SAY THAT WE ARE?
Christian Identity in a Multi-Religious World

WCC Publications is the book publishing programme of the World Council of Churches. Founded in 1948, the WCC promotes Christian unity in faith, witness and service for a just and peaceful world. A global fellowship, the WCC brings together 345 Protestant, Orthodox, Anglican and other churches representing more than 550 million Christians in 110 countries and works cooperatively with the Roman Catholic Church.

Opinions expressed in WCC Publications are those of the authors.

Scripture quotations are from the New Revised Standard Version Bible, © copyright 1989 by the Division of Christian Education of the National Council of the Churches of Christ in the USA. Used by permission.

Cover design, book design and typesetting: Michelle Cook / 4 Seasons Book Design

Cover image: "The Good People Beach Walk," 32 x 48 in., by Texas artist Laurie Justus Pace "through the inspiration and spirit of God the Father." Used with permission. Visit http://www.ellepace.com/.

ISBN: 978-2-8254-1675-4

World Council of Churches
150 route de Ferney, P.O. Box 2100
1211 Geneva 2, Switzerland
http://publications.oikoumene.org

Contents

Foreword

The title of this report deliberately echoes Jesus' words to his disciples in the synoptic gospels: "Who do you say that I am?" Jesus' question leads the disciples to a new step in their faith and their realization of Jesus' identity.

Just as it was then with Jesus and his first friends, so it is today with us: Christian identity and self-understanding are realized not through assertions but through questions. It is our neighbours of other religions who can help us discover who we really are.

The report itself, *Who Do We Say That We Are? Christian Identity in a Multi-Religious World*, is the result of considerable work and widespread collaboration over a period of more than twelve years, which has finally come to this fruition, having been received by the World Council of Churches central committee in July 2014.

The study process which eventually resulted in this document first started in 2002, with a recommendation by the WCC central committee to the three staff teams of Faith and Order, Inter-religious Relations, and Mission and Evangelism, and their respective commissions or advisory bodies. Around this time the substantial document *Ecumenical Considerations for Dialogue and Relations with People of Other Religions* was published. *Ecumenical Considerations* was seeking to ask questions about the rationale and parameters for dialogue with people of other religions; the present document is seeking to offer something rather different (though obviously related), namely, how the living reality of being a Christian in a multi-religious world may, and perhaps should, affect our understanding and perception of our own Christian faith. The premise that underlies the report is that through dialogue with people of other religions we can deepen our understanding of key tenets of our Christian faith, and discover new and fresh insights.

Back in 2003, while working for the Anglican Communion with responsibility for interreligious dialogue, I was invited to participate in the meetings that marked the beginnings of this process. It was the first occasion on which I myself worked with the World Council of Churches. Over the years since, I was also invited to contribute to a number of the "religion specific" consultations that also fed into the development of the present document. So it felt both an honour and a challenge that, when I started working at the WCC myself in 2011 as Programme Executive for Interreligious Dialogue and Cooperation, I was asked by colleagues to draw the process to a conclusion. I am delighted to make it more widely available now in this trade edition.

Clare Amos
Programme Executive, Interreligious Dialogue and Cooperation
World Council of Churches

Who Do We Say That We Are?

Introduction

1. Human beings live in a world of many different faiths, many different religions. In truth, this has always been so, but developments throughout the 20th century and now into the 21st century facilitating speed of communication and travel, together with changes in the political order and large-scale migration, have brought home to many this reality in a way that they would not previously have imagined, or perhaps even desired. Such realization of the religious plurality of our world can provoke a variety of reactions among Christians. These can include wonder, challenge, hostility, embarrassment, puzzlement, self-questioning, and fear.

2. Jesus once asked his disciples the question: "Who do you say that I am?" (Mark 8:29 and parallels). Today, mindful of the religiously plural contexts in which Christian life and witness are set within our world, we ask of ourselves: "Who do we say that we are?" Christians in every age have implicitly asked this question, for it is the point of deep self-reflection where, taking seriously the contemporary needs of witness and mission, we discover whose we are and whom we serve. Our answer to this question both reflects and guides the way we live out our unique religious identity and calling.

3. Christianity itself came to birth in a lived experience of a world of religious plurality. The very earliest expressions of

Christian self-understanding emerged as Christians began consciously to define themselves first as a sect within Judaism and then, partly due to interaction with the pagan world, as distinct from the Jewish faith. "It was in Antioch that the disciples were first called Christians" (Acts 11:26). This primary and fundamental stage in the development of Christian self-identity undoubtedly took place partly because Antioch was a city both famous and infamous for the religious diversity it accommodated. Throughout the first four or five centuries of its life, the church continued to be shaped by its interaction with the Jewish and Hellenistic (Greek) religious traditions, as well as by religio-political concerns of the Roman Empire. The doctrinal developments during this period, culminating in the classic Christian understandings about the nature of God and the person of Christ as articulated in the Niceno-Constantinopolitan Creed, were influenced by a positive implied conversation with the Greek worlds of religion and philosophy. But during the lengthy following period of "Christendom," particularly in parts of the world where Christianity was the dominant faith, politically and religiously, the focus was rather on intra-Christian discussion and argument, which, with occasional exceptions, did not overtly seek to take seriously the faiths and beliefs of others outside the Christian fold. Certainly these others were not normally perceived as influencing how Christians thought about themselves, even though in parts of the world, such as the Middle East, substantial Christian communities lived alongside adherents of another faith for many centuries. During the 19th and the earlier part of the 20th century, the Western missionary movement found itself in situations of engagement, and sometimes conflict, with other religions. Though there was a gradual shift in mission thinking, with many mission practitioners and thinkers becoming committed to constructive dialogue with followers of other religions, the awareness only gradually dawned that such engagement could even impinge upon Christian identity itself. It was only slowly that the insight expressed in the preface to the "Christian Presence" series of books began to filter consciously into the thinking of mainstream Christianity: "When we approach the man [*sic*] of another faith than our own it will be in a spirit of expectancy to find how God has been speaking to him and what new understandings of the grace and love of God we may ourselves discover in this encounter."[1]

4.   Over the last 25 years, and particularly since the beginning of the 21st century, political, ideological, and religious shifts have given a new edge to the need for Christians to engage appropriately with religious plurality. There are at least two complementary aspects to this engagement. One is the importance of enabling constructive dialogue with adherents of other religions. *Ecumenical Considerations for Dialogue and Relations with People of Other Religions*, a document produced by the World Council of Churches (WCC) in 2004, expresses the parameters and principles for such dialogue. There is however another further aspect, perhaps even more urgent, foreshadowed in the "Christian Presence" series, and which the Christian churches and people cannot avoid exploring more deeply today: namely, how a real awareness of this context of religious plurality may affect questions of Christian identity and self-understanding. It is this concern that the present document seeks to address.

---

1. The *Christian Presence* books were a series published by SCM in the 1950s and 1960s. Each book in the series reflected on Christian engagement with a specific religion. The preface (from which the quotation above comes) was written by Max Warren.

5. These early years of the 21st century seem to be marked by a profound dialectic that is affecting the life of our globe. The increasing interaction brought about by travel, communications, and migration has led on the one hand to a deeper sense of shared humanity, and therefore of universal and world-wide concerns, but on the other has also provoked a greater insistence upon particularity and otherness. Religion is not vanishing, as had been suggested by modern predictions of secularization, but rather it remains a vibrant element shaping and influencing culture and civil society. However, religions seem to exemplify fundamental tension. There is both the recognition of the universality of religious experience and commitment, but also the establishment of more rigid boundaries between religions, in part influenced by long histories in which economic, political, and social factors; ethnicity; and demography have all played key roles. As a result, mutual perceptions and relations between religions are frequently dictated by preconceived ideas and a lack of mutual listening.

6. The identities of Christians across the world and their relationships with others are enormously varied as well. They have been shaped by long and diverse processes of interaction in which missionary work has played what sometimes seemed to be an ambiguous role. Many Christians acted out of their faithfulness to the gospel; struggled in humility to share the love, grace, and mercy of God in Christ with other people; and showed genuine solidarity with the marginalized. Yet Christians have often dismissed people belonging to other faiths as merely "heathen" and were far from taking seriously their religious and spiritual traditions. Though stemming from a sincerely held belief in the absolute and exclusive truth of the Christian faith, a pernicious attitude of

cultural superiority had detrimental effects on those others and betrayed the core message of the gospel. Consequently, a critical reassessment of our self-understanding is badly needed. And, indeed, conscious efforts in interreligious dialogue, both locally as well as internationally, have given us a new awareness that relating interreligiously may belong integrally to our Christian identity: it is a vital aspect of the boundary-crossing nature that is written in to the fabric of Christianity. In turn, this must entail an attentive and open listening to people of other faiths.

7.   Our primary identity as Christians lies in the fact that we are "people of the resurrection." Alongside the diversity that marks out Christians throughout the world, we must affirm that this is a common character that binds us together as Christians. From earliest times of Christian history, the followers of Jesus have seen their central role as being "witnesses of the resurrection" (Acts 1:22). It is only in the light of the resurrection that the whole of the Christian story can be fully understood: "He [Jesus] ordered them to tell no one about what they had seen, until after the Son of Man had risen from the dead" (Mark 9:9). The ecumenical movement is founded on the conviction that such a common identity exists within the undoubted diversity of our confessions and cultures. Yet the resurrection is not simply ours, as Christians, to possess. The resurrection of Christ is intimately connected to the resurrection of the whole of humanity. It is no accident that the resurrection accounts of the gospels have an elusive, mysterious quality to them, illustrative of God's refusal to be trapped into particular religious systems or expectations. The resurrection both ratifies the pre-Easter ministry of Jesus described in the gospels, and also throws it excitingly open to the whole world. The WCC general

assembly in Porto Alegre (2006) devoted a plenary session to the question of Christian identity and religious plurality. With respect to the former, it was suggested that our identity of Christians requires us to "carry the name of Christ,"

> to belong in a place that Jesus defines for us in his very person. By living in that place, we come in some degree to share his identity, to bear his name and to be in the same relationships he has with God and with the world ... Christian identity is a faithful identity, an identity marked by consistently being with both God and God's world.

Paul introduces his hymn on the self-emptying of Christ (Phil. 2:5–12) with the exhortation, "Have the same mind in you that was in Christ Jesus." Sharing his "mind" enables us to share in the same relationship he has with God and also with the world, a relationship characterized by Christ's work and ministry of reconciliation.

> To be a Christian is not to lay claim to absolute knowledge, but to lay claim to the perspective that will transform our most deeply rooted hurts and fears and so change the world at the most important level. It is a perspective that depends on being where Jesus is, under his authority, sharing the "breath" of his life, seeing what he sees – God as Abba, Father, a God completely committed to the people in whose life he seeks to reproduce his own life.[2]

---

2. Rowan Williams, "Plenary on Christian Identity and Religious Plurality," WCC Assembly, Porto Alegre, 2006, at: http://www.oikoumene.org/en/resources/documents/assembly/2006-porto-alegre/2-plenary-presentations/christian-identity-religious-plurality/

8.   If we assume our identity as Christians by seeking to stand where Jesus Christ himself stands, this has profound implications for our relationship with God, the world, and with the whole of humanity. It becomes intrinsic to our understanding of who we are to stand in solidarity "in Christ" with the marginalized and the stranger. The self-reflective question "Who do we say that we are?" cannot be separated from the existential question "What must we do?" In the parable of the great judgment in Matt. 25:31-46, Jesus reveals that he has identified himself with the hungry, the sick, the naked, the prisoner, and the stranger, and his resurrection has ratified that this is where we must stand with him now. As this parable makes clear, if we – and others – desire to share his company eternally, we must accept to be identified not only by doctrines or terminology but by the place where we choose to stand.[3] Such a location is risky, and has porous borders that cannot be sealed.

9.   How does this stance of Jesus affect the relationship of Christians to people of other religions? In 1989, a statement made at the San Antonio conference of the Commission on World Mission and Evangelism (CMWE) said, "We cannot point to any other way of salvation than Jesus Christ; at the same time we cannot set limits to the saving power of God."[4] It is with such a "mind" as this, which draws together both faithful confidence and openness of vision, that the deepening of our Christian self-understanding in this multi-religious world needs to be explored. Depending upon our specific contexts, such self-understanding may require of us

rowan-williams-presentation?set_language=en
3. It is perhaps significant that in semitic languages the word for "stand" and the word for "resurrection" are closely linked.
4. Wilson, F.R. (ed), *The San Antonio Report. Your Will Be Done: Mission in Christ's Way* (Geneva: WCC, 1990), 32.

repentance, or it may mean that we need to be prepared to offer a risky or prophetic challenge. But it is a "mind" in which humility is vital and that offers no resting place for arrogance. The word "deepening" is used deliberately because when we open ourselves to people of other religions, we may sometimes hear echoes of what we have come to believe on the basis of our experience of the life, the cross and the resurrection of Christ, and be given fresh insights into our own faith. The challenge for Christians in this world of religious plurality is perhaps to be "re-evangelised through a gracious encounter with other people ... [so that] Christians have been evangelised by people of other faiths – not with another *evangelium*, but with the Gospel of Jesus Christ."[5]

10.   So in responding to the challenges offered to us by other faiths and their peoples, Christians are not only answering queries and critiques posed by our religious interlocutors, we are also rethinking, re-interpreting, and reformulating the understanding of our own faith in a way that is congruent with the tradition of Christian self-reflection and theological development that has existed since the very beginnings of Christianity. This is, of course, a mutual process, and just as Christians may be transformed by their encounter with the religious other, so authentic interreligious engagement may also pose to such others challenges which can lead to transformation.

11.   The following sections of this document explore some key aspects of how Christian identity has been challenged by religious diversity, and how Christian commitment may be nourished by encounters in dialogue with those who do not

---

5. Michael Ipgrave, "Loving Wisdom," unpublished lecture, 2009.

share our perspective and place as they have been defined for us by Jesus in his person. The reflections in these sections take account of the work done at a number of meetings and consultations organized by the WCC over the past decade that have explored Christian self-understanding in the context of a religiously plural world. A note of these meetings is given in the Appendix. The reflections offered are not seeking to collate the reports and findings of those meetings, but rather to use them, as far as appropriate, as a background resource for the current document. We have also drawn, where applicable, on two recent published major documents: *Together towards Life: Mission and Evangelism in Changing Landscapes*, produced by the CWME[6] and *The Church: Towards a Common Vision,*[7] produced by the Commission on Faith and Order, believing that it is important that the interreligious insights offered by the WCC are congruent with recent work offered by these two commissions. As with the document *Christian Witness in a Multi-Religious World,* the current document is intended for a wide audience rather than aimed at specialists in interreligious concerns.

12.   Running through this document, and mindful of the 10th Assembly of the WCC – with its prayer "God of life, lead us to justice and peace" – is the motif of "life." Whatever else our Christian self-understanding in this world of many faiths requires of us, it surely demands that we see ourselves as people who are committed to fullness of life for all. We have become all too aware of the ability of religions, including our own, to become death-dealing rather than life-giving.

---

6. *Together towards Life: Mission and Evangelism in Changing Landscapes, with a Practical Guide*, ed. Jooseop Keum (Geneva: WCC, 2013).
7. *The Church: Towards a Common Vision*, Faith and Order Paper No. 214 (Geneva: WCC Publications, 2013).

The touchstone as to whether or not our self-understanding leads toward life is a vital one, and reiterated by Jesus himself on one of the few occasions in the synoptic gospels when he himself sought to define God: "He is God not of the dead, but the living" (Mark 12:27 and parallels).

13.   A considerable number of Christians, both scholars and practitioners, have been involved in the process that led to this document, and it reflects their vision. All of them, whatever their specific backgrounds and contexts, would acknowledge the critical importance of serious engagement by Christians with people of other faiths. They would avow that it is through such long-term and patient exchange over a considerable period of time, giving to and receiving from people of other faiths, that their own self-understanding and sense of identity as Christians have been enriched and that they have felt able to proffer some questions, even "hard" ones, to their companions of different faiths. At a memorial service held in May 2013 for Bishop Kenneth Cragg, whose important role in the establishment in the 1970s of the WCC Programme for Dialogue with Other Living Faiths and Ideologies is widely acknowledged, it was suggested that Bishop Cragg's life and work exemplified the story of the Emmaus road. It was through the willingness of the disciples to travel a considerable distance with a "stranger," through their willingness to ask questions of him and to respond to those he asked, and finally through their willingness to offer hospitality, that "their eyes were opened and they recognized him"(Luke 24:31) in a new light. Can the courtesy and challenge of the story of the Emmaus road and its crucial witness to the resurrection victory of life offer us a pattern in our quest for our own Christian self-understanding in this world of many faiths? As the WCC shapes its work during

the coming years as a "pilgrimage of justice and peace," this journey to Emmaus may offer us a hint of how our vision can be enlarged by a willingness to travel alongside people of other faiths in our mutual human quest for peace and justice.

14.   In the following sections we explore the theological understandings and affirmations that we share as an ecumenical community as we seek to elaborate an answer to that vital question, "Who do we say that we are?" We begin by affirming that our self-identity as Christians in the contemporary world is grounded in our understanding of God as Trinity. This leads us to explore first what it means to speak of God as the creator of all. Next we focus on our understanding of Jesus Christ, who for Christians represents the redemptive life of the world, and in turn then reflect on the life-giving Spirit of God. In each case we sketch our affirmation and note the deepening and discovery through dialogue that is evoked. Following the explication of these trinitarian affirmations, we touch on scripture, the church, and eschatology as leading elements in the quest to express our self-understanding as Christians set within a religiously plural world. The document is not simply linear, but revisits a number of key motifs during the course of our exploration, thus embedding the pattern of deepening through discovery into its own structure.

Our Trinitarian Frame

Key aspects of Christian conviction

15.   "We believe in the Triune God who is the creator, redeemer and sustainer of all life." These words, with which the 2012 WCC affirmation on mission and evangelism begins, make clear our Christian belief that God as Trinity is the source of life. This is the foundation stone of the Christian understanding of God and of God's relation to the world. The basis of faith adopted by the WCC speaks of our "common calling to the glory of the one God, Father, Son and Holy Spirit." We perceive God as Trinity through God's actions in history and on the basis of God's dealings with humanity. Our experience of God is in the richness of the unity of relational diversity.

16.   In God the Father we see divine and caring creative activity and we affirm that God created the whole world and works constantly to affirm and safeguard its life. In God the Son, Jesus Christ, we find the incarnational expression of God's love for the world (John 3:16). Affirming life in all its fullness is the ultimate concern and mission of Jesus, the Christ (John 10:10). In and through him we experience the redeeming activity of God. In God the Holy Spirit, the Life-Giver, we discover and experience the sustaining and empowering life that renews the whole creation (Gen. 2:7; John 3:8). A denial of life is a rejection of the God of life.

Dialogue, deepening, and discovery

17.   Within the history of Christian encounter with other faiths, the Christian belief in God as Trinity has often appeared problematic, particularly in terms of Christian relationships with Islam and Judaism, where it is sometimes presented as a challenge to the unambiguous monotheism of these faiths. For example, the issue is expressed starkly in the Qur'an: "Believe in God and his messengers and do not speak of a 'Trinity' – stop [this], that is better for you – God is only one God."[8] Within the Hebrew Bible, shared by both Jews and Christians, there are instances where monotheism is stated in similarly uncompromising language: "I am the first and I am the last: besides me there is no god" (Is. 44:6). Trinity has sometimes been misunderstood as tritheism, by a number of Christians as well as people of other faiths – or of none.

18.   What should be the Christian response? Some have sought to downplay the understanding of God as Trinity. Even though they may be willing to speak of God as "Father" or "Creator," Jesus Christ as "Son of God," and of the "Spirit of God," they resist emphasizing a sense of inner inter-relationship between the three persons of the Trinity. Perhaps, however, such questioning should instead compel Christians to dig deeper into the sources of our faith, both biblical and historical. We can then discover that, rather than being a hindrance for engagement with other religions, the Trinity, with its affirmation of the importance of diversity in unity and a communion that involves difference, can provide a model for apprehending the divine engagement with the diversity of our world. "The Trinity, far from being a *skandalon* [stumbling block] is rather the transcendental

---

8. Sura 4:171

condition for interreligious dialogue, the ontological condition that permits us to take the other in all seriousness, without fear, and without violence."[9] The Ecumenical Conversation "Exploring Christian Self-identity in a World of Many Faiths" at the 10th Assembly of the WCC reflected on the Trinity as expressing both the "scandal of particularity" and the "gift of divine plenitude," and suggested that Christo-centric biblical texts, which are often seen as problematic for interreligious dialogue, should be read in the light of the spaciousness offered by our trinitarian faith. For Christians to speak of God as Trinity can facilitate an understanding, helpful for engaging with people of different religions, that "Jesus Christ cannot be an exhaustive or exclusive source for knowledge of God."[10] The trinitarian language of *perichoresis* – of the "Triune persons work[ing] in complex movements of dance: embracing creatures, yet letting them exist in their freedom"[11] – offers an evocative image for interreligious dialogue that is yet to be fully explored. Can we suggest, therefore, that through our engagement with other religions, Christians can both be encouraged to a richer and deeper understanding of our trinitarian faith and, through this understanding, discover a vital theological resource and framework for such engagement?

9. K. J Vanhoozer, *The Trinity in a Pluralistic Age: Theological Essays on Culture and Religion* (Grand Rapids, Mich.: Eerdmans, 1997), 70-71.
10. Mark Heim, *The Depth of the Riches: A Trinitarian Theology of Religious Ends* (Grand Rapids, Mich.: Eerdmans, 2001), 134.
11. Joas Adiprasetya, *An Imaginative Glimpse: The Trinity and Multiple Religious Participations* (Oregon: Pickwick, 2013), 182.

Creator of All

Key aspects of Christian conviction

19.   We affirm our faith in the one God who creates and sustains all things; the living God, present and active in all creation from the beginning until the present. It is "vital to recognize God's mission in a cosmic sense, and to affirm all life, the whole *oikoumene*, as being interconnected in God's web of life."[12] With the psalmist we celebrate:

> The earth is the Lord's and all that is in it,
> the world, and those who live in it;
> for God has founded it on the seas,
> and established it on the rivers. (Ps. 24:1–2)

20.   Our affirmation has two distinct but also interconnected aspects to it. We are required to take seriously and honour the inter-relationship of the entire created realm, animate and inanimate. We also acknowledge that the Bible testifies to God as God of all nations and peoples, whose love and compassion extends to all humankind in its diversity, and this raises in an acute way questions concerning the relationship between God and all the peoples of the earth. This acknowledgment is grounded in the understanding that human beings are created in the image of God (*imago dei*). From this we can affirm the dignity and worth of every

---

12. *Together towards Life*, para. 4.

human being and ultimately our Christian understanding of the inherent relationality of the whole of creation (see Col. 1:15).

21.   The importance of treasuring all creation is written into the biblical story. In the first chapter of the Bible it is underwritten by the repeated use of the word "good" to describe all the results of God's creative handiwork. The intimacy of the connection between humanity and the earth is then underscored by the verbal link between 'adam (= human being) and 'adamah (= earth) that dominates Genesis 2–3. The covenant with Noah (Gen. 9:8–17) is portrayed as a covenant with all creation, making it clear that God's care extends well beyond the realm of humanity. As this covenant with Noah was eventually interpreted, it also opened doors to seeing God's "wisdom and justice extending to the ends of the earth as He guides the nations through their traditions of wisdom and understanding."[13]

22.   Thus from biblical times the realization of God's cosmic work in creation has also raised questions about God's relationship to all humanity. As the people of biblical Israel moved from a tribal world view to a profoundly monotheistic conception of God as creator and Lord of past, present and future, so too they began to comprehend that God's care could not exclude those who did not know him by name. The biblical wisdom tradition, a genre that the people of Israel shared with their neighbours in the ancient Middle East and that reflects biblical openness to the insights of other peoples,

---

13. "Baar Statement: Theological Perspectives on Plurality," WCC, 15 January 1990," *Current Dialogue* 18 (June 1990), 3-7. http://www.oikoumene.org/en/resources/documents/ wcc-programmes/interreligious-dialogue-and-cooperation/christian-identity-in-pluralistic -societies/baar-statement-theological-perspectives-on-plurality.

both draws extensively on the motifs of God's work in creation and frequently addresses profound questions that confront all human beings. In the New Testament, Paul's speech on the Aeropagus in Athens also testifies to the link between our acknowledgment that "God made the world and all that is in in it" (Acts 17:24) and the religious longings of all humanity, expressed through the worship of the one whom the Athenians described as "the unknown God" (Acts 17:23).

Dialogue, deepening and discovery

23. Because we believe in God as the Creator of all, as the Word through which all came to be, as the Spirit that is the life of all, it is intrinsic to Christian identity to discern carefully whatever manifestations of the Word's truth and the Spirit's life there may be in creation, including in the diversity of human cultures and religions.

24. History and theology have meant that Christians have not always been aware of the full implications of their faith in God as creator. During the European colonial era in particular, there was both the rape of land and the refusal to value positively the reality of all human beings as created in the image of God. More recently, theologies that explore God's revelation in history have sometimes neglected to understand how God's revelation has been written in the book of creation as well as the book of scripture.

25. The globalized world in which we live today, our increasing recognition of human diversity and plurality, our concern for the fragility of creation, and the lived experience of climate change require us to dialogue with our religious neighbours to deepen our comprehension of what it means

to call God creator of heaven and earth, the one responsible, indeed, for the *oikoumene*.

26.   One important resource for this has been dialogue with the worldviews of indigenous peoples. With respect to the intimate relationship between God and the complex ecological inter-relationships we may call "creation/land/nature," we are challenged by the awareness of indigenous peoples that

> the whole earth is God's temple, and without the earth we are nothing. All sentient life exists in symbiotic relationship upon and within the earth, and the sharp distinction often made in Christian theology between human beings and animals is minimalised. In many communities of indigenous peoples when people want to get close to God they sit on the ground.[14]

In indigenous thinking, the earth is understood as a living body, and therefore a sacred place, often referred to as "Mother." The ecological crisis of our time reminds us to take this notion of the earth seriously as we organize its use and economy. Thus indigenous worldviews are a challenge to Western science as well as to Christian thought and perspective. The understanding of the inherent relationship of people to land that has been a product of dialogue with indigenous peoples is a challenge to the Christian application of stewardship with respect to land. "Our overall moral and spiritual development cannot be separated from our attitude to land. It is essential for human beings to be in harmony with the land."[15]

---

14. Communique of the consultation on Christian self-identity in the context of indigenous religions WCC, February 2012.
15. Ibid.

27.   Dialogue between Christians and people of other religions
        has also shown us how human beings have at all times and
        in all places responded to the presence and activity of God
        among them and have given testimony to their encounters
        with the living God. We take this witness with the utmost
        seriousness and acknowledge that among all the nations and
        peoples, God has never been without witness (Acts 14:17).
        In this process of encounter with our neighbour of another
        faith we experience a common humanity before God who
        created us all.

28.   In turn this affirmation of God as creator of all crystallizes
        the challenge posed by religious diversity. Some Christians
        would argue that since Christian monotheism denies that
        there can be many gods, then other religions must believe
        in something false, and therefore there can be no ground
        for proper dialogue. For others, it poses the challenge that
        these religions must have a relationship to God and a place
        in God's providence and compels us to address what this
        might mean for our theological self-understanding as Chris-
        tians. Equally, this may lead us to contest situations, such
        as in contemporary Malaysia, where, in the controversy
        relating to the use of the word "Allah," adherents of another
        monotheistic religion insist on a privileged right to restrict
        to themselves traditional terminology and language for God.

29.   That God is active as creator and sustainer in the life of
        all peoples leads to the conviction "that God as Creator of
        all is present and active in the plurality of religions." This

                makes it inconceivable ... that God's saving activity
                could be confined to any one continent, cultural type,
                or group of people. A refusal to take seriously the many

and diverse religious testimonies to be found among the nations and peoples of the whole world amounts to disowning the biblical testimony to God as Creator of all things and Father of humankind.[16]

30.   Our understanding of humanity based firmly on the biblical insight that human beings are created in the image of God is widely recognized to have resourced international developments in the field of human rights. The givenness of human dignity implied by the concept of *imago dei* has encouraged the affirmation of the human rights of every person. In the present context it is especially appropriate to note that such rights include freedom of religion and belief:

> Religious freedom including the right to publicly profess, propagate and change one's religion flows from the very dignity of the human person which is grounded in the creation of all human beings in the image and likeness of God (cf. Gen. 1:26). Thus, all human beings have equal rights and responsibilities. Where any religion is instrumentalized for political ends, or where religious persecution occurs, Christians are called to engage in a prophetic witness denouncing such actions.[17]

31.   We are invited to view interreligious involvement, and our commitment to it, as expressing something that is intrinsic to our Christian identity. Such engagement can allow us to discover something new of God's will and way for humanity created in the divine image.

---

16. Baar Statement, sect. II.
17. "Christian Witness in a Multi-religious World: Recommendations for Conduct," WCC, Pontifical Council for Interreliguious Dialogue, World Evangelical Alliance, 2011, Principle 7.

Jesus Christ,
the Life of the World

Key aspects of Christian conviction

32.   We affirm that in Jesus Christ, Son of God and incarnate Word, the entire human family has been united to God in an irrevocable bond and covenant. The saving presence of God's activity in all creation and human history comes to its focal point in the event of Christ. In Jesus' words and action, in his proclamation, in his ministry of healing and service, in his death and resurrection, God reconciled the world to God's self, a reconciliation which cannot be limited to any one community or culture or confined within Christian institutions.[18]

33.   We believe that the Word incarnate in Jesus is actively present in creation and manifest there. Though it may appear that "the saving power of the reign of God made present in Jesus during his earthly ministry was in some sense limited (cf. Matt. 10:23) through the event of his death and resurrection, the paschal mystery itself, these limits were transcended. The cross and the resurrection disclose for us the universal dimension of the saving mystery of God"[19] and are imprinted on creation as the "watermark of divine love."[20]

---

18. Baar Statement, Sect. III.
19. Ibid.
20. Hans Urs von Balthasar, *Love Alone Is Credible*, trans. D. C. Schindler (San Francisco: Ignatius Press, 2004), 142.

34.   Thus we believe that the risen and living Christ can move and be met beyond the bounds of the church's institutions and proclamation. In these ways, our belief in Christ opens us to seek God's presence through the Spirit within other traditions than our own. It is our commitment to the particularity of Christ that leads us to faith in the trinitarian God who is manifest in many ways in the world.

35.   There are many aspects of Christ and Christ's work, and we mention some important ones here, mindful that for each there may be specific points of connection with other religious traditions:

- Christ as priest and reconciler. By taking on our humanity and suffering in solidarity with us, above all in the cross, Christ overcomes the estrangement of our sin and evil. Language of sacrifice, shared especially with the Jewish scriptural tradition as well as some other religious traditions, is one of the ways in which this is expressed.

- Christ as victor over death. In his resurrection Christ opens up an eschatological hope and promise for new life. The messianic dimension to the work of Christ both connects with and challenges Jewish eschatology.

- Christ as teacher. Christ interprets and embodies the way that his disciples should follow. In this respect there are some similarities with the role of the Buddha.

- Christ as one with God. By virtue of Christ's unity with God, the Christian who has communion with Christ shares in the intimacy of that love. In certain forms of

Hinduism, an analogous union and intimacy with the divine is profoundly affirmed.

- Christ as prophet. As Word of God, Christ reveals God's nature and will. Islam explicitly uses the language of prophecy to describe Christ's work.

- Christ as liberator and victim. Christ's identification with the location of the outcast and oppressed links him with those in such locations who struggle for justice, whatever their faith tradition.

36.   The particular situations of Christians or Christian churches may affect the comparative weight they give to each of these affirmations as they seek to inculturate their Christian faith in their own contexts. These contexts may be geographical, social, and political: they can also include the contexts provided by proximity to people of another faith. One of the significant insights offered by ecumenical reflection on mission during the 20th century is the profound link between the incarnation of Christ and the dynamic ability, indeed need, for the Christian faith to inculturate itself in different ways in different places, reflecting our belief that the incarnation is rooted in the whole of life. Although such incarnational inculturation has normally been explored primarily in relation to varied Christian contexts, it is also appropriate to ask whether and how Christ can be inculturated in different interreligious contexts.

Dialogue, deepening and discovery

37.   We know that affirmations such as those listed above about the person and role of Christ can become not only points of contact but also points of difficulty in our dialogue with

neighbours of other faith traditions. Through such dialogue we experience a variety of challenges for understanding our own identity as Christians: challenges in which we see wisdom and truth in these traditions, from which we desire to learn, and challenges that invite us to ask very difficult questions about the basic understanding of our faith. We also acknowledge, however, that there may still be times when we feel that our Christian identity requires us to continue to challenge the beliefs and assumptions of other faith traditions, but through our dialogue we can discover the appropriate and gracious language to enable us to do so.

38.   As there are many facets to Christ's person and work, so too do many challenges arise to these in the substance of different religions. They are rooted in the positive statement of each religion's own paths and teaching, reflections of the tradition's own identities and practices. We do not suggest that any religion formulates its convictions in order to contradict Christian views. Some of these criticisms or conflicts have already been the subject of extensive discussion in interreligious dialogue, providing material that will be helpful for Christian reflection. On many of these questions we also find Christians themselves debating the most appropriate form for the theological convictions at issue. The examples below are only meant to be suggestive of challenges Christians can recognize as deserving their attention, while each could be stated with much more detail. In light of their own religious convictions, adherents of other religions may:

• question belief in Jesus' oneness with God or belief in Jesus' divinity (this is reflected for instance in Jewish and Muslim concerns that these Christian convictions violate the unity and transcendence of God);

- question the partiality and historical particularity of a single divine incarnation, or that Jesus is "the only way" (seen for instance in some Hindu perspectives on Christ);

- define the human condition and need differently than Christians do (seeing ignorance, for instance, rather than sin and estrangement from God as the fundamental problem), and thus viewing Christ's saving work, as Christians understand it, as impossible or irrelevant (as is the case in some forms of Buddhism and Hinduism);

- question Jesus' messianic role and the legitimacy of Christian interpretations of Hebrew scripture central to the Christian understanding of Christ (as is the case with Rabbinic Judaism);

- question the reality of Christ's death or its link to salvation (as is the case with traditional views in the Islamic tradition);

- question the resurrection or its eschatological significance (as with Hindu and Buddhist traditions that understand Christ within the framework of a cycle of birth and rebirth, and different visions of nature and time).

39.   Christians respond to these challenges from differing Christian perspectives on the meaning of Christ's person and work, including the perspectives of different confessional families and of movements like liberation theology and feminist theology. Christians will also respond differently according to their contexts, for instance those who live as a minority among other faiths and those who live in a culturally dominant setting. The investment required in rethinking

Christianity's relation with other religions is higher for some than others. Yet taking seriously the insight that incultura-tion can be an expression of the meaning of incarnation can also deepen and expand the Christian understanding of the person and ministry of Jesus Christ. "Christ's completion ... comes from all humanity, from the translation of the life of Jesus into the life-ways of all the world's cultures and subcul-tures through history."[21]

40.   However Christian self-examination is also required in light of the testimony of people of different faiths around us. It is needed to distinguish an authentic understanding of Christ from the ways in which our theologies of Christ may have been made captive to cultural and colonial forces. This involves a constant return to Christian sources, re-reading them in light of the specific questions of a religiously diverse world. If Christ is God with us, then by that image we know that gracious care and self-giving love should be the terms in which we are to relate to our religious neighbours, even though Christians may struggle to attain such self-examina-tion and such care. In particular the challenges *to* Christian understandings of Christ offered by our religious neighbours can remind Christians that our theologies and forms of proclamation have often blocked us from even considering the value and legitimacy of other religious traditions, and we can discover that the image of a conquering, dominant, and judging Christ has done much damage.

41.   At the same time, our deepened understanding of the nature of Christ may also require us to challenge modalities of power and dominance and their abuse when we find them present

---

21. "The Ephesian Moment," in *The Cross-Cultural Process in Christian History*, ed. Andrew F. Walls (Maryknoll, N.Y.: Orbis, 2002), 79.

in other religions. In contexts in which the Christian community is a vulnerable, and possibly impoverished, minority
living precariously in the midst of powerful religious majority, it is important to speak of life and resurrection as well
as crucifixion and suffering. Great wisdom is needed on the
part of the Christian community in such situations to ensure
that relations between different religions do not spiral into a
vicious circle of increasing hostility and misunderstanding,
while at the same time finding ways to speak with sensitivity
about the liberating gospel of Christ.

42.   Amid the multifaceted ways in which Christ and his ministry can be understood, the affirmation that Christ is "saviour of the world" (John 4:42) assumes particular weight
for many Christians yet can also be particularly problematic
for their religious neighbours, especially if there is the consequent perception that relationship to Christ will be the
sole basis on which all people are judged by God. We indeed
believe that the life and ministry, death and resurrection of
Christ is the fundamental expression of the universal saving
will of God. Yet we affirm again the mystery presented at
the CWME meeting in San Antonio in 1989, "We cannot
point to any other way of salvation than Jesus Christ; at the
same time we cannot set limits to the saving power of God.
... We appreciate this tension, and do not attempt to resolve
it." [22] We see Christ as a specific saving gift to all creation,
not a replacement for or denial of God's presence and power
through many other means. Christ embodies God's generosity toward humanity. Christians point toward this event as
their hope, not toward Christianity as the source of salvation. Christians are called to testify to this hope.

---

22. Wilson, *San Antonio Report*, 32-33.

We need to acknowledge that human limitations and limitations of language make it impossible for any community to have exhausted the mystery of the salvation God offers to humankind. ... It is this humility that enables us to say that salvation belongs to God, God only. We do not possess salvation; we participate in it. We do not offer salvation; we witness to it. We do not decide who would be saved; we leave it to the providence of God. For our own salvation is an everlasting "hospitality" that God has extended to us. It is God who is the "host" of salvation.[23]

Through reflection on our identity in a multi-religious world we discover we need to clarify that testimony and ask: In what ways may we see religions as avenues of God's authentic relation with humanity and as contributing to human salvation? We can also learn that salvation, in the terms that Christians understand it, is not necessarily a common point with those of other traditions. The religions testify to their own ideals and aims – *nirvana*, *moksha*, submission – and describe the paths to attain them.

43.   Christian belief in the unique role and significance of Christ does not deny that other traditions are also unique. There is no direct connection between the affirmation of Christ's unique saving work, on the one hand, and the restriction of salvation to those within the church, on the other. In fact, among Christians there is a variety of views about whether and how God offers salvation through other religions. Our Christian engagement with our religious neighbours requires us to explore more profoundly what we as Christians make

23. "Religious Plurality and Christian Self-Understanding," *Current Dialogue* 45 (July 2005), 4-12.   http://www.oikoumene.org/en/resources/documents/assembly/2006-porto-alegre/3-preparatory-and-background-documents/religious-plurality-and-christian-self-understanding.

of the aims and achievements of the adherents of other traditions. How do we account for their moral and spiritual lives in relation to the triune God?

44.   These challenges do not arise in the abstract but in daily encounter with those in various religious traditions. In turn, our reflection needs to engage the specific issues and sources of particular religions. For instance, when we hear Shi'a Muslims commemorating their martyrs, or hear stories of Bodhisattvas who give their lives for others, we may hear elements that resonate with and perhaps even enrich our understanding of the costliness of God's love and of God's vulnerability in love. We can discover how people of other faiths in some situations seem to arrive at a lively appreciation of their need for God's forgiveness and of the richness of that forgiveness. We recognize that there are those elements in other traditions that immediately enhance or deepen our faith, yet there are others that we experience as critical, even threatening to convictions that we hold dear. An example of this would be the use of power and commitment to physical *jihad* in certain expressions of Islam, which conflicts with the Christian ideal of servanthood. This kind of engagement with the religious others – and with the ways in which we figure as "other" to them – is both risk and vocation, as the WCC central committee noted in adopting the 1979 *Guidelines on Dialogue*.[24]

45.   The importance of challenge as leading to potential discovery applies to all the themes we are exploring in this report. It is however a helpful insight to recall, especially as we explore how religious diversity challenges our understanding

---

24. *Guidelines on Dialogue with People of Living Faiths and Ideologies* (WCC, 1979).

of Jesus Christ, the Life of the World, for it takes us deep into the pattern offered by Christ himself. It may be a risk to develop our self-understanding in partnership with our religious neighbours, in the sense that we cannot put limits in advance to the extent to which our understandings, or those of others, may be changed. But it is also a vocation, rooted in the very heart of our faith, by virtue of our confidence in the universality of Christ and our desire to emulate Christ's openness and love.

Life-Giving Spirit of God

Key aspects of Christian conviction

46.   We affirm that the lifegiving Holy Spirit

> is believed to be active in the Church and the world. The ongoing work of the Holy Spirit in the whole of creation initiating signs and foretastes of the new creation (2 Cor. 5:17) affirms that the healing power of God transcends all limits of places and times and is at work inside as well as outside the Christian church transforming humanity and creation in the perspective of the world to come.[25]

47.   Christians therefore have come to appreciate the manifold and mysterious ways in which God the Holy Spirit is at work in the world and among the peoples. This conviction leads to openness and to an honest dialogue with people of other faiths, cultures, and world views. More specifically we wish to state: "The Holy Spirit is the Spirit of wisdom (Is. 11:3; Eph. 1:17) and guides us into all truth (John 16:13). The Spirit inspires human cultures and creativity, so it is part of our mission to acknowledge, respect and cooperate with life-giving wisdoms in every culture and context."[26]

---

25. *The Healing Mission of the Church*, Preparatory Paper No. 11 for the Athens 2005 conference organized by CWME, para. 40.
26. *Together towards Life*, para. 27.

48.   However, the ministry of God's Spirit is related to the redemption of the whole creation, not to humanity alone (Rom. 8:19–22). Thus Christian spirituality and lifestyle must not be based on the idea of a separation of humanity and creation; humanity is part of creation, indeed a microcosm of it. God indeed seeks the redemption of both, perhaps in varied and mysterious ways.

49.   Recent reflection on the theology of mission and interreligious dialogue has often emphasized the importance of the Spirit, because of the testimony offered by the Bible to the Spirit's universal and unpredictable character, complementary to the particularity offered by the person of Christ. Yet it is also clear that in the New Testament the Holy Spirit can never be dissociated completely from Jesus Christ. It is Jesus Christ, the one who was crucified and resurrected, who breathes the Spirit (John 20:21f) on his disciples. It is in Jesus' name that the Holy Spirit, the Paraclete, is sent (John 14.26). And Jesus' birth (Matt. 1:18–25; Luke 1:35), Jesus' baptism (Matt. 3:17), Jesus' testing in the wilderness (Mark 1:12), and his ministry of healings, exorcisms, and other miracles (Matt. 12:28) are expressions of the Spirit. Indeed the terms Spirit of God/Spirit of Christ/ Holy Spirit can apparently be used interchangeably (Acts 16:6-7; Rom. 8:9).

Dialogue, deepening, and discovery

50.   The increased attention given to the Holy Spirit and the Trinity in ecumenical Christian theology over the past couple of decades has affected Christian engagement with other religions, both theologically and practically. We can think of it in circular terms: our deeper exploration of the Holy Spirit has opened new pathways with our religious neighbours

that have circumvented what has been called the "Christological impasse in the theology of religions."[27] In turn, however, these new pathways have encouraged further Christian discovery of the treasures offered by the Holy Spirit and our affirmation of the trinitarian nature of God, and have brought together Christian scholars and practitioners from a wide range of backgrounds to their mutual enrichment. The phrase "the Go-Between God"[28] used of the Holy Spirit may emphasize the Spirit's role in mediating new relationships, not only between God and human beings but among the divinely cherished diversity of humanity, including its religious dimensions. The CWME meeting in San Antonio expressed it like this: "The Spirit of God is at work in ways that pass human understanding and in places that to us at least are least expected. In entering into dialogue with others, therefore, Christians seek to discern the unsearchable riches of Christ and the way God deals with humanity."[29] We see "the activity of the Spirit as beyond our definitions, descriptions and limitations, as 'the wind blows where it wills.'"[30]

51.   The Holy Spirit has been called "the mysterious one of the Godhead" or "the surprise of God"[31] and can help us rediscover the importance of mystery both in Christian theology and in other religions. This mysterious aspect of the divine is a significant motif in a number of other religions – Islam and Buddhism, for example – and relationships between Christians and members of these religious communities have encouraged Christian awareness of the spiritual value of mystery.

27. T. W. Tilley, "Three Impasses in Christology," *CTSA Proceedings* 64 (2009): 71-85.
28. Used first by John V. Taylor, *The Go-Between God* (London: SCM, 1975).
29. Wilson, *San Antonio Report*, 31.
30. Baar Statement, sect. IV.
31. Von Balthasar, *Love Alone*, 142.

52.   Although we affirm that the Spirit blows where it wills, we
would still confess the relationship of the Spirit with Christ.
In this way,

> a more inclusive understanding of God's presence and
> activity in the whole world and among all people [is
> promoted], which implies that signs of God's presence
> can be found even in unexpected places. On the other
> hand by clearly affirming that the Father and the Spirit
> are always and in all circumstances present and at work
> together with the Word, the temptation to separate the
> presence of God or the Spirit, from the Son of God, Jesus
> Christ, will be avoided.[32]

Indeed, we might well say that whereas Christ is God
incarnate, the Holy Spirit is God enspirited within the world
of God's creation.

53.   Though the Spirit may not be directly knowable, the experience of the Spirit can be known. Looking for signs of the
Spirit the report of the Athens CWME Conference distin-
guished in the Bible four criteria for discernment, although
none of these leads to conclusive identification of the Spirit:

- *ecclesial:* confessing Jesus as Lord (1 Cor. 12:3; 1 John
  4:2). The Spirit can be found wherever Jesus Christ is
  known and worshipped But it is the Spirit that defines
  the church and not the other way round.

---

32. *Mission and Evangelism in Unity Today*, Preparatory Paper No. 1 for the Athens 2005
Conference organized by CWME, para. 12.

- *personal and life-changing:* the evidence of the fruit of the Spirit: love, joy, peace, patience, kindness, generosity, faithfulness, gentleness, and self-control (Gal. 5:22). The Spirit changes our lives, producing Christlikeness. In other words: it is the heart and character that matters.

- *charismatic:* the practice of the gifts of the Spirit (1 Cor. 12:4-11; Rom. 12:6-8). Where there is empowerment to prophecy, ministry, teaching, exhortation, giving, leading, compassion, and so on, we have good reason to believe God is at work (by the Spirit). However exercise of a spiritual gift is not a sign of the Spirit's presence if it lacks love (1 Cor. 13:1-3).

- *ethical:* being on the side of the poor. The effect of the Spirit's anointing on Jesus Christ was that he preached good news to the poor (Luke 4:18) and this must be a touchstone for all claims to be filled with the Spirit. When discerning the Spirit in any Christian activity, we need to ask whose interests are being served; who is benefiting from this?[33]

54.   The question remains open whether all of these criteria or any of them alone can be applicable to the discernment of the Spirit's work in other religions. When applying any of these criteria we also have to ask the question of love that for Paul is the ultimate criterion (1 Cor. 13), even beyond faith and hope. Taking this list of criteria seriously, we see there is a double aspect: it offers us the possibility of positive

---

33. See Kirsteen Kim, "Come, Holy Spirit": Who? Why? How? So What?" in *Come Holy Spirit, Heal and Reconcile!* ed. Jacques Matthey, Report of the WCC Conference on World Mission and Evangelism, Athens, Greece, May 2005 (Geneva: WCC Publications, 2008), 155f.

discovery of the richness of the Spirit's presence in and out-side the church, including in creation. However, the second aspect is that the Spirit may be absent, whether from our-selves or from religious others, where we thought the Spirit would be present. The claim that the Spirit is with us is not ours to make; it is for our neighbours to recognize.

55.   A further unresolved question is whether we understand the world as being moved by one spirit (of God), or whether we acknowledge the activity of multiple spirits – perhaps both good and evil. In the world view of many people of other religions and among some Christians, there is a belief in the reality, agency and presence of spiritual forces ("principali-ties and powers"), which affect humanity and the world in an essential way. These forces can have life-affirming or life-destroying power. Indeed, for many Christians the encoun-ter with evil in the world is experienced as an encounter with spiritual powers. However, in the case of a world view with multiple spirits, we must not treat people of other religions as being necessarily moved by evil spirits.

56.   Yet we need to ask: What is the relationship between such many spirits and the one Holy Spirit? What are the impli-cations of the Holy Spirit in a world of violence, racism, exclusion, natural catastrophes, and other causes of major suffering or injustice? For the hope that is in us compels us to say that the Holy Spirit is no tranquilizer to give us peace that puts us to sleep[34]: the Spirit comes to transform our world and enable a new creation.

---

34. The image is drawn from Samuel Rayan, *Breath of Fire* (London: Geoffrey Chapman, 1979).

Scripture, Written That We May Have Life

Key aspects of Christian conviction

57. We seek to be a community living in obedience to Jesus Christ, the eternal Word of God who is revealed through the words of Holy Scripture. We discern the voice of the living God in our scripture. In both Old and New Testaments we repeatedly find a link being drawn between God's scriptural revelation and the sources of life (e.g., Ps. 19:7; Ps. 119:77, 93; John 20.31; Rev. 20:12). All Christian churches have a high regard for scripture, which is referred to as the foundational witness of God's revelation. In its capacity as a normative guide and rule for the Christian faith community, the Bible has an enduring authority. In many Christian communities it also functions as an object of veneration in a liturgical context.

58. The Bible tells the unfolding story of God, creation, and humanity. It bears testimony to the universal nature of God's love. Christians embrace the biblical story as their own, as being formative for their self-identity. In the light of a tradition they have received from the past, Christians not only interpret and give meaning to their present lives but also envision a future that finds its fulfillment in God.

59. The Bible is a library of books, containing a variety of genres: narratives, prophecies, wisdom literature, proverbs, legislative texts, parables, hymns, and so on. This inner

diversity points to the diversified ways in which humans have experienced and expressed their relationship with God. The Bible has not only emerged but has also been received and interpreted differently in various social, historical, and cultural contexts. Therefore Christians struggle to negotiate the tension between the claim that the Bible has a universal and univocal scope and the recognition of the contextual specificity of both its origin and its ongoing interpretation. With regards to biblical interpretation, Western culture has in the past assumed that the historical-critical approach to interpretation should be normative for all Christians. This assumption is now rightly under critique.

60.   The church submits itself to being interpreted by the ever-challenging revelatory word of God. At the same time, the church is also called to interpret anew the word of God in rapidly changing circumstances and in light of always new challenges and does so by using a variety of interpretative strategies. History testifies to the fact that this ongoing process of reinterpretation has given rise to many intra-Christian conflicts. So there is the task of overcoming misunderstandings, controversies, and divisions; identifying dangers; and resolving conflicts. The nature of the intricate relationship between the Bible and the church is a theme that many Christian confessions continue to wrestle with.

61.   An issue that reveals divergence within the Christian community between different confessions is the question of precisely which biblical books should be regarded as canonical. In some cases this raises particular doctrinal challenges. What this means for Christian self-understanding as living under the authority of scripture is an issue in ecumenical

dialogue. In terms of interreligious engagement it may, for example, raise issues for discussion about the nature and authority of the Christian canon.

Dialogue, deepening, and discovery

62.   The contemporary experience of religious diversity challenges Christians to reflect upon their self-understanding as a community that needs to take seriously the interpretation of scripture.

> Our presence in, and engagement with, multi-religious contexts lead us to read the Scriptures in new ways. We come to recognize that the people of God have already known and grappled with the challenges and opportunities of living amid religious plurality, and that those experiences have shaped the formative texts of Scripture ... As the people of God today, we can find the biblical text coming to life in a new way as we engage in our discipleship with issues which raise questions similar to those they faced. For many [Christians] ... the Bible speaks with immediacy and clarity into their contemporary situations of inter-religious encounter.[35]

This is a process that may involve both the encounter with the sacred scriptures of other religions and a re-engagement with the Bible and its interpretation.

63.   "Almost all of the major religious traditions have scriptures either written down or transmitted in oral tradition. These scriptures are often seen as sources of their faith, and often

---

35. *Generous Love: The Truth of the Gospel and the Call to Dialogue* (London: Anglican Communion, 2007), 5.

as directly revealed by the Divine."[36] That is why they are not only regarded as authoritative, but also as sacred and holy. Because these scriptures are considered to be sacred, they are treated within their communities with the utmost respect and reverence. Sometimes they even function as objects of veneration. Often there are rules about who can read these scriptures and how these scriptures can be interpreted. For Christians, particularly from the Western world, the physical respect given to these scriptures can be an educative experience, which challenges us to consider, in turn, the care with which we should treat our own sacred texts.

64.   In the case of a number of religions, their scriptures privilege the particular language in which they were originally written down or transmitted. In some cases this means that these scriptures are formally untranslatable – for example the Qur'an cannot be read in its fullness in any language other than Arabic. Although Christians consider the original biblical languages of Hebrew, Aramaic, and Greek as being important for the study of scripture, there has normally been an acceptance of the validity of linguistic translation of the Bible. An awareness of this different attitude to text and translation can encourage Christians to explore more deeply what exactly is meant by biblical inspiration, and opens doors to potential reflection on the parallel between translation and incarnation that has been suggested by scholars and practitioners of mission, who have spoken of the "translation principle" being intrinsic to Christianity.[37] What does it mean to say that the Bible becomes the life-giving word of

---

36. Wesley Ariarajah, *My Neighbour's Faith and Mine: Theological Discoveries through Interfaith Dialogue* (Geneva: WCC, 1986).

37. E.g., Andrew F. Walls, "Incarnation Is Translation… Christ, God's Translated Speech Is Re-translated from the Palestinian Jewish Original," *"The Translation Principle" in the Missionary Movement in Christian History* (Edinburgh: T & T Clark, 1996), 27.

God because it is translated in many languages to be received by many people?

65.   Though their adherents do not explicitly recognize it, the scriptures of many religions came to final form most usually as the result of long and often complex processes of formation. This process quite often also entailed borrowing from other religious wisdom traditions as well as polemical apologetics reacting against other religions. Realization of this can encourage Christians to re-read their own Bible and become more sensitive to similar interplays within it as well. Linked to this may be also the potential for further reflection on the relation between scripture, tradition, and the life of the community of faith. The reality that, unlike in Christianity, a number of other religious communities consider reading and studying the sacred scriptures a prerogative of the elite can constitute a challenge to Christians engaged in inter-religious dialogue. It can also encourage them to look at the Bible with new eyes.

66.   Of particular importance is the relationship between the Christian scriptures and those of Judaism and Islam, the other two so-called Abrahamic faiths. In the case of Judaism and Christianity, the two religions share part of their scripture. With regard to Islam and Christianity, the relationship is not so close, but the appearance of a number of the same figures in both the Bible and the Qur'an raises questions about the historical and theological relationship between the Christian and Muslim scriptures. The issue of supersessionism, particularly vis-á-vis Judaism and Christianity, is raised by the scriptural relationship between these two religious communities; the New Testament's apparent suggestion that the Old Testament has now been fulfilled,

or perhaps even superseded, challenges Christians to rethink anew the fraught history of their relationship with Judaism. But the implicit supersessionism of the Qur'an with regard to the "People of the Book" confronts Christians with similar questions, this time issued to them through the scripture of another religion. However, such scriptural overlapping offers possibilities as well as problems. The recent development of the process of scriptural (or textual) reasoning, in which Muslims, Jews, and Christians share together in the reading of each of their scriptures, offers participants the opportunity to deepen the knowledge of their own scriptural tradition as well as to be enriched by the interpretation of others. Christians who have participated in interreligious scriptural reasoning have witnessed how, through such re-reading, they may discover their own faith through the eyes of another: one's own faith loses its self-evidence and can be rediscovered anew.

67.   The document *A Common Word*[38] provides a significant illustration of the potential linkage between scripture and interreligious engagement. The authors argue that for both Muslims and Christians, love of God and love of neighbour are core beliefs, which can be used as a springboard for dialogue enabling Muslims and Christians to work together for the common good. The Christian text chosen to illustrate love of God and love of neighbour is Jesus' discussion of the great commandment in the law (Matt. 22:34–40 and parallels), in which, of course, Jesus himself also expounds scripture. Thus, through *A Common Word*, an interreligious aim encourages Christians to reflect on a specific biblical passage with special seriousness, perhaps

---

38. Issued in November 2007 as an invitation to Christian leaders and scholars by a group of Muslim scholars linked to the Royal Aal Al-Bayt Institute in Jordan.

even inviting Christian readers to encounter the passage in a new light.

68.   Although the Bible does not directly address interreligious dialogue as it is understood and practiced today, there are certainly passages in the Bible that can be read in ways which can provide positive resources for interreligious encounters. The idea that Christians can learn about God through the encounter with the religious other is not foreign to the Bible. As in the case of a number of other areas (gender, race, etc.), the urgency of interreligious encounter has provided the impetus to highlight particular threads within biblical material. The following examples are illustrative rather than exhaustive:

- The three magi from the East who made use of their own astronomy and religious insights to find the newborn baby Jesus and to worship him (Matt. 2:1–12).

- The encounter between the Syrophoenician woman (Mark 7:24-30; see also Matt. 15:21–30) and Jesus. This woman demands that Jesus pay attention to her and that he not limit his mission to the Jews. As the story is told in the gospel of Mark, the woman seems to break through Jesus' religious and cultural prejudices and make it clear to him that God's love and care extend beyond those of Jesus' own people. "The woman taught Jesus how to be Jesus" (Hisako Kinukawa). In the story, Jesus shows himself open to change. Such openness to change rests on a great trust in God. Jesus discovers, it seems, how God addresses him in a person who does not belong to his own faith community. God himself is at stake for Christians in interreligious dialogue. It is God who challenges us.

- The conversation between Jesus and the Samaritan woman recorded in the gospel of John (John 4:5-42). This, the longest conversation Jesus has with any one individual in the gospels, is remarkable as an example of Jesus' engagement with religious otherness in a variety of ways. In particular there is Jesus' surprising response to the Samaritan woman's religious question about the "right" place to worship: "Our fathers worshipped on this mountain, but you Jews claim that the place where we must worship is in Jerusalem" (John 4:20). If he had chosen to answer her question from within his own religious tradition, Jesus' response would have been to assent that the temple in Jerusalem was the correct place for worship. But John surprises us by representing Jesus as someone who was well aware of his own tradition and yet was able to rise to a spirituality of religious awareness that was called for in that particular inter-religious-intercultural encounter. Jesus answers, "Yet a time is coming and has now come when the true worshipers will worship the Father in spirit and truth, for they are the kind of worshippers the Father seeks. God is spirit, and his worshipers must worship in spirit and in truth" (John 4:23–24). Not only is Jesus able to rise above the cultural and religious givens of his own community, but it is especially significant that someone from outside that community appears to be the catalyst in this process. We thus get a glimpse within scripture of how interreligious engagement can be a source of rethinking self-understanding.

69.   These three examples suggest that it is the content as well as the nature of the Bible that offers scope for deepening Christian self-understanding in the encounter with

religious diversity. It is notable that these three examples each come from a different gospel (Matthew, Mark, John). In each case, and perhaps particularly in the final example from the John, we hear the distinctive note of the particular gospel-writer, who is seeking to share the story of Jesus in a way that meets the needs and concerns of his own specific readership. How far is this redactional process on the part of the gospel-writers helpfully illuminated by reading these stories in the context of interreligious diversity? What light does this shed on our understanding of the nature of scripture? In turn, how far can this redactional process itself offer insights for a religiously plural world? The writers of the patristic era considered it significant that there are four canonical gospels: Does this model of diversity in unity itself offer a resource for engagement with other religions?

70.   One issue that cannot be forgotten when reflecting on the Bible in the context of religious diversity is that of "toxic texts": passages that seem to promote violence or xenophobia as divinely sanctioned or encourage abusive attitudes to human beings on the grounds of gender, ethnicity, or social status. Interreligious engagement has forced us as Christians to become more aware of such passages and has made it more difficult for us to ignore them in a conspiracy of silence. (That is also true in relation to other religions and similarly difficult texts in their scriptures.) We have had to address some hard questions. However, as part of wrestling with these passages, awareness is increasing that the fundamental hermeneutical principle for scripture is to be life-affirming, taking seriously the purpose statement offered near the end of the gospel of John that "these things are written ... that

you may have life in his name"(John 20.31).[39] This is the perspective from which our biblical interpretation needs to proceed.

---

39. See for example the WCC Global Theological Platform statement in 2008 on "The Bible, Crisis and Catastrophe." The platform analyzed the use and interpretation of biblical texts in relation to three key issues: climate change; Christian Zionism; and HIV/AIDS. See http://www.oikoumene.org/en/resources/documents/wcc-programmes/unity-mission-evangelism-and-spirituality/just-and-inclusive-communities/global-platform-on-theological-reflection-and-analysis-2008

The Church, Called Out for Life

Key aspects of Christian conviction

71.   Within the ecumenical family we have a broad spectrum of church understanding: as a gathered community of the faithful (*koinonia*); prophetic, priestly, and royal people of God; body of Christ and Temple of the Holy Spirit; etc. The church today acknowledges and honours the "people of Israel" (Rom. 9:4) as God's chosen people from whom the church has derived elements of its self-understanding and "to whom God will always remain faithful."[40]

72.   The church exists within the tension of universal and particular. The very idea of "church," however theologically formulated, can be expressed in terms of a generic or universal concept on the one hand, and manifest as a concrete historical fact, bound by time and space, on the other. The concept of "church" presupposes the doctrine of "the One Holy Catholic and Apostolic Church." The contemporary ecumenical context of church life challenges us to resolve the gulf between the manifest plurality of churches and the ideal, already proleptically realized, of oneness in Christ. Even so, we are aware this is an eschatological hope for which we work. The lived reality is in the tension between unity and diversity. Thus the ecumenical experience of being "church"

---

40. *The Church: Towards a Common Vision*, para. 17. This text is extensively drawn on in this section even when it is not directly quoted.

provides a reference point for understanding, appreciating, and acting upon what it means to be church in the context of religious plurality. In the encounter with other religions we need to be mindful of key aspects of self-understanding and consequent challenges. In the paragraphs below we draw attention to some significant aspects.

73.   The church is understood as "elected" (Eph. 1:4), that is, chosen by God and assigned a divine purpose and identity. The church reflects the trinitarian life of God; it is a community grounded in love and expressing the relational nature of her creator. The church is itself a unity of diversity, the church of the triune God. The church is also a narrative community, that is, whatever our particular ecclesiology, in belonging to a church we locate our Christian identity within a set of narratives that include the Bible (and especially the passion narrative), church history and tradition, our local and particular stories of discipleship, and church life – and much more besides. The church includes saints and sinners. It is both a divinely created reality and a human organization whose members are all "saved sinners" engaging in God's mission of love, charity, and sacrificial service. The church's true life involves the proclamation of the good news of salvation, and thus evangelical activity, administration of sacraments, diaconal service, and mission in the way of Christ.

74.   The church is the locus of Christian identity, both personal and communal. It is for some the means of salvation, for others, the setting for outworking the life of discipleship. Either way, there is an intimate and necessary relationship between the life of faith as a personal concern and belonging to the church as communal expression and faithful responsibility. Furthermore, while Christ is the eternal head of the church,

there are also various structures and systems of authority and accountability whereby order is maintained through which the life of the church is sustained.

75.   The church is also the springboard for proclamation and evangelization, as an aspect of God's mission in the world. Matthew 28:19–20 situates the resurrection commission of Jesus to "make disciples of all nations, baptizing them in the name of the Father, and of the Son and of the Holy Spirit, and teaching them to obey everything that I have commanded you" in the life of the ecclesial community in which Jesus promises to be present with his followers "to the end of the age." The church is called by Christ in the Holy Spirit to witness to the Father's reconciliation, healing, and transformation of creation.

76.   "Rooted in the plan of the Triune God for humankind's salvation"[41] and brought to birth at Pentecost, ever enlivened and inspired by the Spirit, there is a broad spectrum of what it means to be church represented in the ecumenical family. Linked to our wide range of understandings of "church" are also diverse understandings of the kingdom of God – on the one hand seen as a description of church; on the other hand the realm of God's activity that is other and greater than church. In this latter definition, the kingdom of God is the realm that the church is called to serve. Within the wide ecumenical range of church understanding and practice, the sacraments of baptism and eucharist serve as criteria for inclusion and exclusion, with varying emphasis within and between denominations.

---

41. Ibid., para. 3.

Dialogue, deepening, and discovery

77.   The interaction of the church with the plurality of religions raises a number of points for reflection. The church is not simply about doctrine and belief; it is about love in action and about relations of service and love in respect to ourselves and our neighbours. To the extent the church may be open toward the religious other, how are dialogical openness and proper identity as church kept in balance?

78.   The presence of other religions challenges our Christian identity whenever the church portrays itself as an exclusive community in such a way that the exclusivity is perceived not as attractive uniqueness but rather as forbidding exclusion. The historic claim of the church that *extra ecclesiam nulla salus* ("there is no salvation outside the Church") can constitute a "scandal" (stumbling block) for our religious neighbours. On the other hand, if we believe that where the Spirit is, there is the church of God, then if the Spirit appears outside what we understand as the boundaries of the church, we may need to reflect on whether the canonical and spiritual bounds of the church necessarily coincide. Religious diversity has encouraged Christians to explore more deeply the parameters of inclusivity and exclusivity in the life of the church. This can be expressed at a number of different levels, physical and practical as well as theological and spiritual.

79.   Our understanding of "church" encompasses not only spiritual and relational or community meanings and aspects, the term "church" also refers to physical space, as itself both a real and a representative presence; the place not only of worship activities but also of hospitality and sanctuary. Thus a question arises: To what extent is the church a hospitable space? Is it a "barrier" or a "meeting ground"? How we conceive

and construct our church buildings as places of exclusive or inclusive activity is also challenged by the presence of the religious other today. The high sacramental moments of baptism and eucharist, on the one hand so significant for Christian life and self-understanding, can on the other hand make clear for us our exclusion of the religious other. Similarly, other ritual practices, adorning art, and use of liturgical vestments can serve as markers of exclusive identity that are likewise challenged, especially in contexts of multi- or cross-religious pastoral situations. The realm of hospitality offers one area where Christians can be "re-evangelized" by their religious neighbours: for example, the experience of hospitality received from others – a tradition of particular importance in the Sikh religion where the house of worship or *guru-dwara* (literally "the door of God") offers nourishment to all to demonstrate the abundant generosity of God – can help Christians come to understand more deeply the importance of hospitality as part of the church's participation in God's mission.

80.   Today there are many new forms of being church, for the most part aimed at transcending traditional barriers and advocating the widest possible inclusion. This can extend into the interreligious arena as when people of other faiths may participate, or at least attend, various liturgies (marriage, baptism, and so on). The question is raised how far it is right to seek to be inclusive by modifying theological language and ritual practice. On the one hand, the church is challenged to meet real pastoral need and seeks to reach out, and accommodate, ever-greater diversity; on the other hand, the church needs to safeguard the essential integrity of the expressions of faith in language and liturgy. There are increasing signs in many parts of the world that people,

otherwise members of or adherents to the church in its local context, may also find themselves engaging in the ritual and practical life of another religious tradition, by virtue perhaps of mixed-faith family circumstances, for example. The boundaries demarcating religious identity may be increasingly fluid. The phenomenon of Christians holding to some form of multiple, or at least dual, religious belonging and participation is not only a challenge for the mission of the church but also very much a challenge to Christian self-understanding of "church" in today's religiously diverse world. If church authority is being challenged by signs of fluid religious boundaries, is the correct response to advocate a hardening of borders and an exclusionary withdrawal from an interfaith arena, or to deepen the relational engagement and re-consider what the Spirit is saying to the church in such situations?

81.   Our varied interreligious contexts also invite us to reflect on the relationship between the church and evangelization, and that between evangelization and dialogue. "Sharing the joyful news of the truth revealed in the New Testament and inviting others to the fullness of life in Christ is an expression of respectful love,"[42] which needs to be carried out respectfully. In certain interreligious situations, the saying traditionally ascribed to St Francis of Assisi, "Preach the gospel at all times, if necessary use words," may become a vital maxim in the life of the church. Churches in some contexts may find themselves needing to address varied questions about the relationship between *diakonia* and evangelization in their ecclesial lives. These might include to what extent acts of service and justice can appropriately replace evangelization

---

42   Ibid., para. 60.

as a focus in the life of the church, but also require questions to be asked to ensure that there are no inappropriate forms of allurement linking evangelization and *diakonia*. Additionally, if we believe that our Christian faith requires of us dialogue, engagement, and sensitive mutual witness with those of other faith traditions, then shaping the life of the church within wider society to facilitate this becomes important. What shape this might be varies from place to place: in countries with a Christian majority there may need to be overt expressions of hospitality toward other faiths; in countries in which Christians live as a minority, the role of the church to advocate courteously for its members may be required.

82.   Religious diversity also compels us to wrestle seriously with the sometimes ambiguous relationship between the church and the kingdom of God. If the kingdom of God is other than the church, and is understood as the realm of God's activity within the world to which the church is called to engage with and on God's behalf, how then do we understand the role of the religious other within that world? How do we see God relating to the world? If, indeed, the church does not possess God (which it does not), then the prospect that God is at work in and through the religious other cannot be dismissed and must, instead, be a fulcrum point for Christian self-reflection on the nature of the church. Part of the tension within which the church stands today is the perennial issue of the right relationship between the church and the world – within which there are to be found our neighbours of other faiths and of none, all of whom are part of God's creation and all of whom are loved by God. God does not only express love through the church and Christian salvation but rather acknowledges all truth, justice, value,

and excellence, even in contexts that are not immediately within the realm of the Christian community (Phil. 4:8: "whatever is true, whatever is honourable, whatever is just, whatever is pure, whatever is lovely, whatever is commendable, if there is any excellence, if there is anything worthy of praise").

83. One aspect of the relationship between the church and the world that may be challenging in various situations of religious diversity is the link between religious communities and the state. In a number of countries where the population is predominantly Muslim, for example, there is a bond between the state and the religion of Islam, which means that the "world" represented by the state assumes a religious hue, though not a Christian one. In some cases, this is directly linked to the self-understanding of Islam. Conversely in many countries of Europe, the historically privileged position of one or more of the Christian churches can also mean that that secular space has shrunk in other directions. Sometimes the church may need to ask hard questions of itself; sometimes it may also need to ask hard and challenging questions of its religious neighbours. The relationship between the church and the world and our aspiration for an inclusive and hospitable church can feel unrealistic in situations in which Christians are experiencing discrimination or even persecution from religious others. If positive interreligious engagement can affect our Christian theology, self-understanding, and sense of identity, the converse is also true.

84. The special relation between the church and the Jewish people from the beginning poses a particular theological challenge and raises the need for re-thinking our self-understanding.

If the church has not replaced the "people of Israel," what now is the proper link to them? Relations with the Jewish people constitute a very special and particular dimension of Christian interreligious engagement. The church has ever had to wrestle with the presence of Jewish people and the faith of Judaism, and has come to recognize that, in fact, the covenant made between God and Israel continues as much with the Jewish people as it does with those who follow Christ. In the out-working of the rethinking and new self-understanding that Christianity has engaged in, especially since the mid-20th century, there can be found paradigms and possibilities for Christian self-understanding in respect to the presence of, and engagement with, other faiths. The church's relation with the Jews is not a problem; it is part of the answer of what it means for the church to co-exist in God's diverse world with those not of our faith.

85.   The church is one; it is also many. The historical reality of Christianity is to exist in many different forms of church. This is the reality that the ecumenical movement arose to address, wrestle with, and overcome. The horizon of ecumenicity is the eventual organic unity of all Christians in one holy catholic and apostolic church community. The lived reality of ecumenicity is the fostering and development of the ties of affection and bonds of mutual understanding and acceptance; we have learned to live, work, and worship together, even though we cannot yet gather around the same table. We are still challenged by our own diversity and what that means for our self-understanding as Christians. Yet the resources and lessons we have learned along the way may also provide resources and the basis for rethinking what the fact of wider religious diversity might mean for Christian self-understanding. Where previously we erected barriers of

disavowal and mutual denial, we have found God working in and through each other and have been challenged to expand our horizons of theological self-understanding. The inter-religious context is not the same as the inter-church one, but there are some parallels and similarities of relational dynamics and the challenge to understand the working of the God who is Lord of all in this, as much as it is the case to grasp what God is saying to us even in and through our Christian diversity. The ecumenical journey may itself encourage and inform us as we seek to reflect on the meaning of "church" in a context of religious plurality. Equally the need for Christians to engage with wider religious diversity may strengthen the ecumenical movement, for the task of such engagements perhaps too big for a divided church.

Eschatology, Hope for Life

Key aspects of Christian conviction

86.   Eschatology, with its perception of God working out a purpose throughout time, is intrinsic to the Christian faith. A focus and concentration only on present realities, with no sense of future hope or judgment, ultimately diminishes the richness of Christianity. Eschatology, however, is frequently misunderstood or parodied as only focusing on the "four last things": death, judgment, heaven, and hell. Although eschatology certainly includes the exploration of these topics, it is much wider in scope, wrestling with the totality of God's action in history and eternity. Eschatology in Christian terms has a personal, a communal, and a cosmic aspect. There is development within scripture about eschatology – both on a personal level (e.g., life after death) and on the cosmic level (the perfection of God's purpose in creation). Even within the New Testament there is divergence in eschatological viewpoints (compare for example the apocalyptic millenarian vision of Revelation and the "realized eschatology" of John) – particularly in response to the question of the delay of the Parousia or Second Coming of Christ. This plurality of views in the New Testament is an important feature that it is important to allow to find expression also in post-biblical Christianity.

87.   There is an interplay in eschatology between the material and
spiritual as well as the present and the future. In Christian
history sometimes one aspect is emphasized – sometimes the
other. Both, however, need to be held in tension. In personal
terms, overemphasizing the spiritual dimension can lead to
a focus on "immortality" at the expense of "resurrection."
In communal and cosmic terms, focusing on certain aspects
of eschatology can lead to down-playing the importance of
issues such as wellbeing and justice in our world: because we
are "looking for life after death" or "the end of the world,"
we cease to care about well-being in the present. It is therefore important to hold onto the vision of the kingdom of
God which characteristically does not speak of present/
future as either/or but as both/and, with a future continu-
ally becoming present. When we pray in the Lord's Prayer,
"Your kingdom come," we are both offering ourselves to be
agents of the coming of the kingdom and (in the doxology)
acknowledging that God's kingdom is "for ever and ever."

88.   In our religiously diverse world some aspects of eschatological faith appear particularly significant:

- We know that to contemplate the realization of God's
reign is to look "through a glass dimly" and that we cannot
adequately conceive of the fullness of redemption. Faith
kindles in us a recognition that this reality will be wider,
deeper, and more wonderful than we can imagine. Therefore, in the area of eschatology we are particularly aware
that we know only in part and look forward to the light
to come.

- Though we cannot claim to understand God's coming reign in all its fullness, we believe that whatever the

dimensions of the new creation, it will always reflect the trinitarian revelation of God and the loving communion of God with creation that we know in Christ.

- Belief in the radical goodness of the eschatological future is the great reservoir for Christian visions of social change and justice. The contrast between the world as it ought to (and will) be and the world as it is provides us with the basis for critique, hope, and change. This faith in God's future leads us to work against existing evil and commit ourselves to goods not yet present.

- In the eschatological fulfilment we will "know as we are known," and have the deepest possible communion with the trinitarian God. In history we know God through the economy of God's action, encountering God as creator, God in Christ, God through the Spirit. The economic activities of God are truly distinct, even though in each case it is the fullness of God in three persons who is manifest, even when humans perceive God in a limited perspective.

- There is a tension in Christian eschatological thinking between a belief in *apokatastasis*, the fulfilment of God's purpose in all things, and a belief in consummation as involving judgment and division, heaven and hell. This can also be seen as a tension between hope for the salvation of all persons and the reality of the possibility of damnation or annihilation. Consummation will be like a great feast in which all the nations come from east, west, north, and south. It will also be like a judgment in which we are divided based on whether we served the "least of these" as Christ (Matt. 25:31–46). There are also varieties of views relating to possible intermediate states of human beings between death and their ultimate destinies (such as purgatory).

- We believe that the life, death, and resurrection of Jesus Christ mark a turning point in history, the decisive entry of God's eschatological future into our human story. The salvation constituted by Christ is the same as the reign of God that is fulfilled at the end of days. That salvation has come in Christ and awaits its full consummation. It is already real and it is not yet completed. This is why Christians await Christ's return. Salvation is a relation of communion with other creatures and with God through unity with Christ.

- The realization of the reign of God is fulfilment of God's purpose for creation. Just as in the present time the faithful live by "remembering" this coming consummation and its character, so is the past renewed. The book of Revelation echoes the book of Genesis, and the Sabbath is both a recollection of God's resting at the close of creation and foretaste of the life to come. Christ is a second Adam, and in him all past humanity is caught up. This is expressed in the confession that at the time of his death and resurrection, Christ descended to bring with him the faithful of prior ages.

Dialogue, deepening, and discovery

89.   Some in other religions object to Christian eschatology because they see it as an arrogant and presumptuous claim to judge other peoples and religions and to determine their ultimate fates because of supposed absolute knowledge about God's will and the future. It is important for Christians to

remember that "Eye hath not seen and ear hath not heard, neither hath entered into the heart of man the things God has prepared for those who love him" (1 Cor. 2:9). Eschatology makes us keenly aware of the great scope of God's new creation and of the limits of our perception. This suggests there is room for reflection with our religious neighbours: that our present differences and conflicts may be changed when what is hidden is revealed. This prompts humility and openness toward those of other faiths, and hesitancy to render final judgments.

90.   Even the universalist strands of Christian eschatology could be said to be problematic: Is it a sort of arrogance to offer a universalistic vision centred on the cosmic Christ to those who may not wish to recognize Christ as Saviour? Are other traditions allowed their own integrity and treated in terms consistent with their own self-description? Is their clear witness to their own uniqueness, and their considered rejection of Christian confession respected? Such challenges to Christians have in turn encouraged more profound reflection on the trinitarian nature of God, suggesting that eschatological fulfilment will encompass a unity in diversity of creatures, their proportionate participation in the life of God who is a communion of persons. All creatures will share in that communion through their own uniqueness. These different members of the body of Christ together share greater breadth of God's glory than any could alone. This leads us to ask how the religious identities and particularities of humans might be brought into that communion. May the integrity of diverse faith backgrounds endure in varied forms of participation in this consummation? Will there be distinctive Jewish faith in heaven? Or is heaven beyond all faiths such as we know them?

91.   Conversely, some religions also offer a challenge as to whether Christian eschatology downplays the goodness and importance of the present creation, over-emphasizes the spiritual at the expense of the material, flies from engagement with the world, focuses on the world to come or apocalyptic narratives rather than on human need, and encourages an attitude that does not take seriously enough questions of justice. However, the eschatological expectation of a "new creation" for all can be the ground for common cause with those of other religions in struggling against whatever threatens the well-being and flourishing of creation. It is also grounds for us to learn from other traditions about aspects of that goodness that we may miss.

92.   In Christian iconography and religious art the most usual depiction of the "last things" portrays the last judgment in a manner recognizably linked to the parable of the sheep and the goats of Matthew 25:31–46. In this parable, the criterion for salvation and judgment is notably not linked to confessed faith but to actions of common humanity and justice. Yet the link made between the recipients of the actions and the figure of Christ also jars and unsettles the reader, whether professedly Christian or an adherent of another faith. Christians need to place themselves with the outsider in order to place themselves with Christ; for religious "others" there is Christological meaning imposed on their own acts of service. The parable is a paradigm of a discomfort that leaves no one unchallenged.

93.   Some other religions differ explicitly over whether there is any ultimate being, over whether a personal God exists, and over the terms of human estrangement and fulfilment. Some, for instance, do not share the broadly linear concept of

history that is part of the framework of the Abrahamic faiths and certainly Christianity. Rather, they have a more circular view. This leads (e.g., *karma*, *nirvana*) to a radically different understanding of life after death, resurrection/immortality, and the destiny of the world. The predicament of humanity and humanity's solution are seen to have a timeless character; history itself is part of the problem, and the eschatological belief in the redemption of history is problematic. Once again, this may encourage us to find a resource in our trinitarian faith. Since this faith requires us to recognize that God is manifest in diverse ways – for instance in the call and word of God to Israel, in the incarnation in Christ, in the gifts of the Spirit – it may be possible to respect also the diversity of manifestations of God within other religions. Believing that these manifestations stem from the trinitarian God, Christians may see that they represent authentic contact with God for those in these traditions, and that other religions have much to teach us about specific dimensions of relations with God.

94. Eschatology focuses in an acute way the essential challenge of religious plurality to Christianity, namely the relationship between universalism and particularism, between the hope that God wills all to be saved and the possibility of eternal separation from God. Are other religions entirely occasions for judgment and division, or can they be instruments in God's universal saving purpose? Is lack of faith in Christ cause for eternal punishment? Can those who maintain their devotion to other religions be saved? This tension between universalism and final division has long been perceived by many Christians, quite apart from the challenge offered today by our multi-religious world. Indeed, the modern reality of religious diversity requires us to more clearly address

this ancient question, compelling us to contemplate whether religions play a role in God's universal plan, and to consider the place of those who do not confess Christ yet serve him in their obedience to God's will and their mercy toward their neighbours and the oppressed. We must avoid making belief in God's justice and judgment an instrument in human conflict and religious polemics, or deploying the notion of judgment as a way of condemning our religious neighbours. We may also ask whether the various intermediate states after death (such as purgatory) described in some Christian traditions play any role in relation to other faiths or to the various post-mortem states envisioned in those traditions.

95.   Christians focus their view of the world to come around Christ and the conviction that the reign of God has become real in Christ. Those practicing other religions challenge this connection because they fail to recognize it and reject the idea that the eschatological age has already begun with the incarnation. For instance, among the challenges presented to Christianity by Judaism is the Jewish concern that the messianic hopes for peace and justice, linked by Christians to the person of Christ, have not yet been fulfilled in Christ's coming. Eschatology expresses our recognition that the world is not yet transformed in such a way as to make salvation in Christ obvious. It enables us to join with those of other faiths in recognizing all that "groans in travail" in our world while awaiting redemption. Thus, for instance, it makes possible a convergence with the Jewish critique of absolute Christian claims of fulfilment. Those Jews who await a messiah and Christians who await the return of their messiah can agree on the gap between the present and the messianic kingdom.

96.   For Christians, salvation is offered by the incarnation, which is the unique expression of God's saving will and is realized in a life of unity with Christ. In respect of the testimony of our religious neighbours, and in faithfulness to our own witness, we acknowledge that salvation and the ultimate ends sought by other religions are not the same things. Interreligious dialogue makes clearer to us the specificity of the gospel we proclaim, and its hope of salvation. Such dialogue or mutual witness can likewise make us aware when the specific ends sought in other traditions diverge from salvation. Such ends (*moksha, nirvana*, emptiness) may be real possibilities. If so, how shall we understand them?

Conclusion

97.   "Who do we say that we are?" The question of our Christian
        self-identity is related to the question of Jesus to his disci-
        ples: "Who do you say that I am?" – which comes (quite lit-
        erally) at the heart of the gospels. In particular, the exchange
        between Jesus and his disciples is located in the very middle
        of the gospel of Mark (Mark 8:29). It is preceded by a nar-
        rative that generates a sense of mystery and slowly builds up
        to Peter's startled realization of Jesus' messianic identity: it is
        followed by the second half of the gospel, which leads Jesus
        toward Jerusalem – city of suffering and glorification – but
        at the same time explores what this identity means for his
        disciples. And in terms both of what it meant for Jesus and
        what it means for his friends, it becomes clear that tradi-
        tional understandings are being subverted. So when we ask
        the question, "Who do we say that we are?" as we "carry the
        name of Christ,"[43] we find ourselves uncomfortably stand-
        ing in the place of a figure whose own self-identity has con-
        founded expectations.

98.   "Who do you say that I am?" Is there a possible hint or allu-
        sion in this question to the divine "I am" that, first intro-
        duced in Exodus 3:14 to enable liberation from slavery,
        reverberates from Old Testament to New and offers us both

43. Rowan Williams, "Plenary on Christian Identity and Religious Plurality," WCC Assembly,
Porto Alegre, 2006.

challenge and mystery, encouraging us also to move from a simplistic Christocentrism to the gift of the Trinity? "I am who I am" – the assertion through which God, in addressing Moses, offers a definition of the divine name, presenting us with revelation in apophatic terms, an enigmatic God who cannot be reduced to an object. "Revelational but not telling everything ... disclosing intimacy, personal presence, but preserving mystery, forbidding possession and control?"[44] And if this is true for the time of revelation in the Old Testament, might it also be true for the divine disclosure in the New?

99.   It is well known that in the gospel of John, Jesus repeatedly claims for himself the divine title, "I am." The moment in that gospel when the expression is first used, however, is not generally so well-known. It comes in John 4:26 – toward the end of Jesus' conversation with the Samaritan woman, when Jesus says to her, "I am, the one who is speaking to you."[45] It is notable that this occurs at the end of a fairly lengthy conversation in which, beginning with their discussion of the basic human need for water, the woman and Jesus, representing different religious communities, have covered the range of their respective religious particularities. In 4:23–25, Jesus' language suggests that these differences – which had caused considerable hostility between Jewish and Samaritan religious communities – can now be overcome. Intriguingly, as he makes this point in the conversation, he refers to both "Father" and "Spirit" in terms that suggest that it is the nature of God as Trinity to transcend the causes of religious tension. And then, in response to the woman's comment

---

44. Eugene H Peterson, *Christ Plays in Ten Thousand Places* (Hodder & Stoughton, 2005), 157, 159.
45. NRSV translation, "I am he, the one who is speaking to you," in Greek *ego eimi*.

about the coming of the Messiah, Jesus goes on to claim identity not only with the promised Messiah but, through his use of the mysterious "I am," with the God who has to be worshipped in spirit and in truth. We can genuinely say, therefore, that the initial divine disclosure of Jesus in the gospel of John is prompted by an interreligious conversation. We must also acknowledge, however, that this disclosure has an aspect of mystery.

100.   "Are you the one who is to come, or are we to wait for another?" (Matt. 11:3–4; see Luke 7:20–22) Jesus answers this question, asked by the disciples of John the Baptist, with another question: "What do you see me do?" before going on to demonstrate that "the blind receive their sight, the lame walk, the lepers are cleansed, the deaf hear, the dead are raised and the poor have good news brought to them." Identity cannot be separated from action. Who we are is validated by what we do, no less for us than for Jesus himself.

101.   "Who do we say that we are?" The multi-religious realities of our world today may seem to some Christians jarring and disorienting. Yet at the same time, such a conversation with our fellow human beings of other religious traditions can enable us to discover and disclose new insights into the nature of our ongoing Christian conversation with God. This is the God whose story is one of dialogue and engagement with human beings from the beginning of life and creation, and who has promised that space and eternity will never be able to separate us from the breadth of divine love.

Recommendations

Given the importance of an informed and appropriately confident understanding about Christian self-identity, particularly in contexts of religious plurality, those responsible for preparing this document for consideration by churches, national, and regional confessional bodies and mission organizations recommend that these bodies undertake the following:

R.1. Initiate study processes on the questions and issues raised in this document, taking specific account of their particular context and tradition, and share their responses with the WCC. Such exploration will involve reflecting on past and present understandings of our Christian identity, exploring how our identity has shaped, both positively and negatively, our actions and our engagement with our religious neighbours. Such articulation has the capacity to enliven and deepen our theological self-understanding.

R.2. Develop creative ways to introduce the material to a wide range of people, in particular those involved in teaching and training. This may involve cross-cultural and cross-regional ecumenical dialogue and exchange, so that individuals and communities can learn from a variety of different contexts.

R.3. Encourage their members to deepen their knowledge and understanding of different religions. Such education ideally includes the holistic dimension of meeting people, reading their holy texts, visiting their places of worship, and offering and receiving hospitality. It will be aimed at enabling Christians to be more sensitive to the internal diversity of other faiths and religions. It will also foster a spirit of honesty, so that people compare like with like, not judging the best in their own religion alongside the worst in the religion of another.

R.4. Explore ways to work together ecumenically to respond to initiatives from people of other faiths, drawing on what, as Christians, they are able to affirm in common.

R.5. Build links between people of different religions and faiths who share perspectives and interests in common. For example, groups of women from different religions might study together to deepen their critical understanding of the role of patriarchy in their respective faiths.

R.6. Cooperate with members of other faiths and religious communities in actions aimed at fostering justice and the common good, remembering always the biblical injunction to "seek the welfare of the city in which you are to be found" (Jer. 29:7). Such cooperation might lead to specific projects in which Christians and members of other religious communities work "side by side."

R.7. Work together with members of other faiths and religions to create a climate in which "face to face" dialogue is facilitated. What precisely this means may differ from context to context, but the encouragement of a spirituality of dialogue is normally an appropriate expression of Christian identity.

R.8. Pray for their neighbours and their well-being, recognizing that prayer is integral to our identity – to who we are and what we do.

Appendix – Background to the Document

1. Religious plurality, and its potential for contributing to both peace and hostility in our world, is an issue that has marked out the early years of the 21ˢᵗ century. Bearing this in mind, the central committee of the WCC, at its meeting in 2002, suggested that there should be a study process on the subject of religious plurality and Christian self-understanding, taking account of the experiences of churches all over the world living in varied contexts of religious plurality.

2. In order to address the different dimensions and aspects of the theme, the networks of the WCC's departments of Faith and Order, Mission and Evangelism, and Inter-religious Dialogue engaged together over a period of two years (2003-2004), and at the end of this period scholars linked to these networks produced the document *Religious Plurality and Christian Self-Understanding*. This document was discussed at a hearing session of the central committee in 2005, and at the World Mission Conference and at the Standing Commission of Faith and Order, both held in the same year. Though the document was welcomed by many, a number of the comments made confirmed the view that there needed to be further reflection on this theme. The document however served as a background resource at the 9ᵗʰ Assembly of the

WCC in Porto Alegre in 2006, where the importance of the theme and the desirability for further work were confirmed.

3.   This led to a number of "religion specific" consultations during the period 2008-2012 that explored Christian self-understanding in the context of one particular religion or religious tradition. These consultations focused respectively on Islam (2008), Buddhism (2009), Judaism (2009), Hinduism (2011), and Indigenous Religions (2012). These consultations were organized by the WCC's Programme for Interreligious Dialogue and Cooperation. The papers and discussions of these consultations have fed into the ongoing process. Additionally, the document "Christian Witness in a Multi-Religious World: Recommendations for Conduct," published by the WCC, the Pontifical Council for Interreligious Dialogue, and the World Evangelical Alliance in June 2011, has been a resource for the process.

4.   This document, "Who Do We Say That We Are? Christian Identity in a Multi-Religious World," therefore seeks to draw together the reflections and work of the last decade. It has been drafted as a result of a gathering of scholars held at the Ecumenical Institute, Bossey, Switzerland, in March 2012, and a further meeting held at the Desmond Tutu Centre, Nairobi, Kenya, in February 2013. The meetings were held under the auspices of the WCC's Programme for Interreligious Dialogue and Cooperation, but intentionally also included individuals linked to the Faith and Order and Mission and Evangelism networks.

5.   A draft of the document was then used as a background resource for the ecumenical conversation "Exploring Christian Self-Identity in a World of Many Faiths," held during

the 10th Assembly of the WCC in Busan, Korea, October 30 – November 8, 2013. Insights from that conversation fed into its final revision, which took place in March-April 2014. The document was presented to, and accepted by, the central committee of the WCC, which met in July 2014.